BEWARE!

KILLER PLANTS

BURNING PLANTS

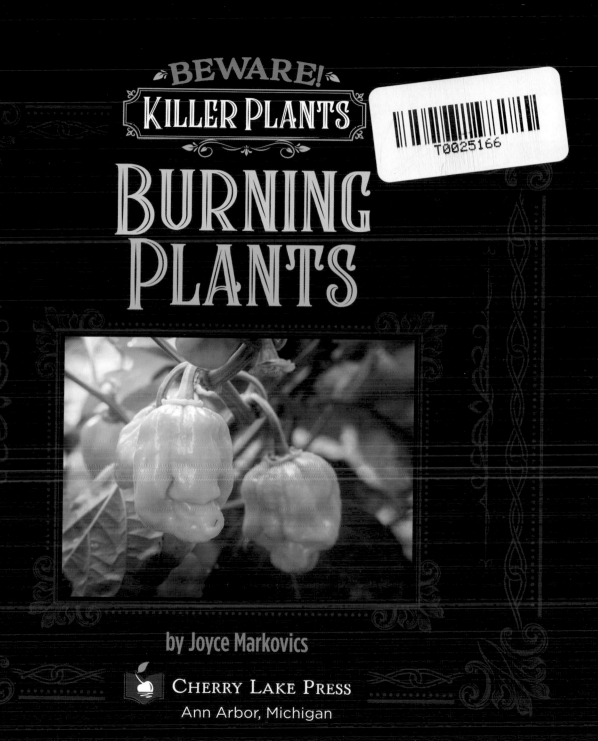

by Joyce Markovics

CHERRY LAKE PRESS

Ann Arbor, Michigan

CHERRY LAKE PRESS

Published in the United States of America by Cherry Lake Publishing Group
Ann Arbor, Michigan
www.cherrylakepublishing.com

Reading Adviser: Beth Walker Gambro, MS Ed., Reading Consultant, Yorkville, IL
Content Adviser: Angie Andrade, Senior Horticulturist, Denver Botanic Gardens
Book Designer: Ed Morgan

Photo Credits: © BDKKECO72/Shutterstock, cover and title page; © Marijs/Shutterstock, 4; Wikimedia Commons, 5; © viicha/Shutterstock, 6–7; © Tanya Kalian/Shutterstock, 8; © freepik.com, 9; Wikimedia Commons, 9 bottom; © SpeedKingz/Shutterstock, 10; © Silarock/Shutterstock, 11; © freepik.com, 12; © freepik.com, 13; Jörg Hempel, Wikimedia Commons, 14; Wikimedia Commons, 15; © Mark Atkins/Shutterstock, 16; © Kazakov Maksim/Shutterstock, 17; © suradech sribuanoy/Shutterstock, 18–19; © Galyna Andrushko/Shutterstock, 19 bottom; © yoko_ken_chan/Shutterstock, 20; © SoniaDigital/Shutterstock, 21; © Blair Costelloe/Alamy Stock Photo, 22.

Library of Congress Cataloging-in-Publication Data
Names: Markovics, Joyce L., author.
Title: Burning plants / by Joyce Markovics.
Description: Ann Arbor, Michigan : Cherry Lake Publishing, [2021] | Series:
  Beware! killer plants | Includes bibliographical references and index. |
  Audience: Grades 4-6
Identifiers: LCCN 2021001249 (print) | LCCN 2021001250 (ebook) | ISBN
  9781534187702 (hardcover) | ISBN 9781534189102 (paperback) | ISBN
  9781534190504 (pdf) | ISBN 9781534191907 (ebook)
Subjects: LCSH: Poisonous plants—Juvenile literature. | Dangerous
  plants—Juvenile literature.
Classification: LCC QK100.A1 M3734 2021 (print) | LCC QK100.A1 (ebook) |
  DDC 581.6/59—dc23
LC record available at https://lccn.loc.gov/2021001249
LC ebook record available at https://lccn.loc.gov/2021001250

Printed in the United States of America
Corporate Graphics

CONTENTS

Hogweed Horror

Jayden Bird won't soon forget a family camping trip in England. The young boy could be scarred for life. On a sunny day in 2020, 9-year-old Jayden brushed against a huge plant while playing in a field. Little did he know that his leg had touched giant hogweed, one of the world's nastiest plants.

Giant hogweed can grow more than 15 feet (4.6 meters) tall!

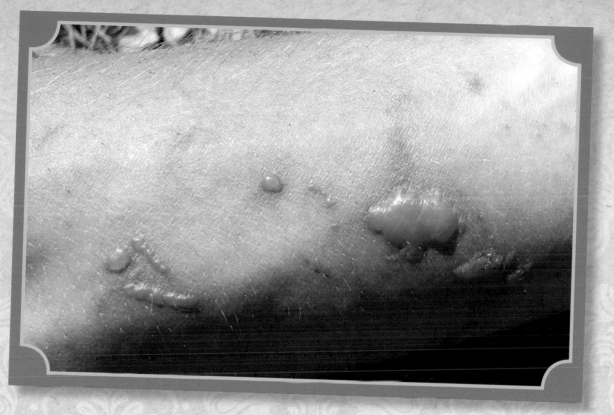

Blisters from giant hogwood

Within a day, round **welts** appeared on Jayden's leg. They grew large and painful. After a couple of days, the red marks became burnlike **blisters**.

WARNING: Plants can be deadly. Never touch or eat an unfamiliar plant.

Jayden's family rushed him to the hospital. Doctors treated him for a giant hogweed "burn." He learned that the sap of the plant can be very harmful. When **exposed** to light, the sap is powerful enough to destroy skin cells.

Giant hogweed is a member of the carrot family. The plant uses its sap to defend itself against hungry animals.

The sap of the giant hogweed plant is **phototoxic**. It causes what looks to be a bad burn on the skin. If the sap gets into a person's eye, it can even cause blindness. Jayden was lucky to escape with only a minor injury.

If you come into contact with giant hogweed, wash your skin with soap and cold water. And stay out of the sun!

DEATH BY PEPPER

Giant hogweed is one of many plants that can burn. Some peppers are so hot that they can send a person to the hospital. In 2016, a man took part in a chili pepper eating contest in New York state. He gobbled down a Carolina reaper, one of the hottest peppers in the world.

Carolina reaper peppers

After swallowing the pepper, the 24-year-old man was sick to his stomach. Then his brain felt like it was being stabbed with a hot knife. This kind of severe head pain is known as a thunderclap headache.

Wilbur Scoville

A pepper's spiciness or heat is measured on the Scoville scale. The scale was named after scientist and pepper lover Wilbur Scoville.

The pepper eater was taken to a hospital. When doctors scanned his brain, they found an issue. His blood vessels were very narrow, causing the awful headache. But what had caused the blood vessels to shrink in the first place?

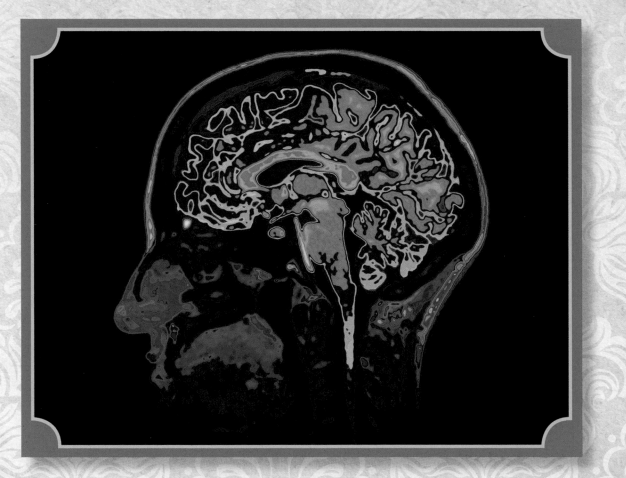

A scan of the human brain

The doctors decided that the Carolina reaper pepper was to blame. A chemical in very hot chili peppers can cause blood vessels to narrow. The same thing happened to another man after eating spicy peppers. However, that man died.

In 2016, a man coughed so hard after eating a chili pepper that he ripped a hole in his throat.

Just a small number of peppers are dangerous to eat. Many, such as bell peppers, are harmless and mild tasting. Spicy peppers contain **capsaicin**. In people, capsaicin tricks the brain. It causes a burning feeling in the mouth but does not actually burn.

Bell peppers can have a sweet taste.

Capsaicin is used for other surprising things. Gardeners use it to deter pests, such as mice. It's even used to stop elephants! Farmers in Africa apply capsaicin to their crops to keep elephants from eating them.

People also use capsaicin on their skin to relieve muscle pain.

BURNING BUSH

One plant burns in an entirely different way. It catches fire! The gas plant is related to orange and lemon trees. In summer, the plant oozes an oily liquid that smells similar to ripe lemons.

The gas plant grows in Europe, Asia, and Africa.

Like the giant hogweed, the oils from the gas plant can **irritate** the skin. But even stranger, the oils can burst into flames. Why? They contain isoprene, a highly **flammable** chemical.

The gas plant is also known as the burning bush.

If the air gets hot enough, the gas plant's oils can **ignite**. Or if someone lights a match near the plant, it can easily catch fire. However, the oils burn off quickly and do not harm the plant. But why does the plant go up in flames at all?

The gas plant can start a fire in an area.

Scientists learned that isoprene can protect the plant from drying out on hot summer days. But they're exploring another possibility. The gas plant might be trying to destroy nearby plants. These plants could compete with it for water and other resources.

In spring, the gas plant is covered in pink flowers.

FIRE GRASSES

Cogon grass is a plant that burns as well as cuts. Each blade of the yellowish-green weed is covered with tiny crystals. Together, the crystals form a jagged, knifelike edge. The blades are so sharp they can cut a cow's lip or a person's skin.

Cogon grass has an even more powerful weapon—fire. Cogon grass is flammable even when it's green. After it catches fire and burns, the plant grows new, stronger shoots and roots.

Cogon, or kunai, grass grows worldwide. In Asia, it's used to thatch roofs.

Another fire-loving plant is pampas grass. The grass grows in huge clumps with feathery stalks. The massive plant can reach 10 feet (3 m) high and 6 feet (1.8 m) wide. Pampas grass is not just large, it's highly flammable.

A clump of pampas grass can produce hundreds of thousands of seeds. The seeds are often spread by the wind.

Fire does not kill pampas grass.

When pampas grass ignites, it burns hot and fast. The plant has been known to fuel huge wildfires. As a result, Americans are trying to eradicate it. "Remove it before it can spread and cause harm," said one plant expert.

Pampas grass comes from the pampas, a large, treeless area in South America. It now grows across much of North America.

PLANT PARTNERS

Plants and animals sometimes help one another. This type of relationship is called mutualism.

Hoverflies are honeybee look-alikes. Like bees, they visit pepper flowers to feed on nectar and pollen. As they do, the flies pollinate the flowers. Hoverflies also lay their eggs on pepper plants.

Serrano Pepper

The pepper plant has colorful, sweet-smelling flowers that attract hoverflies. The flowers produce nectar for the flies to feed on.

Hoverfly

Hoverflies pollinate the pepper plant flowers, helping the plant reproduce. Young hoverflies eat aphids that attack the plant.

GLOSSARY

blisters (BLISS-turz) fluid-filled swellings on the skin

blood vessels (BLUHD VESS-uhlz) tiny tubes, such as veins, that carry blood around a person's or an animal's body

capsaicin (kap-SEY-uh-suhn) chemicals in pepper plants that can cause a burning feeling

compete (kuhm-PEET) to struggle against others to gain something

deter (dih-TUR) to prevent or discourage something

eradicate (ih-RAD-uh-kayt) to get rid of something completely

exposed (ek-SPOHZD) not protected from or left uncovered

flammable (FLAM-uh-buhl) able to catch fire easily

ignite (ig-NITE) to catch fire

irritate (IHR-uh-tate) to cause discomfort

massive (MASS-iv) giant or huge

nectar (NEK-tur) a sweet liquid produced by plants

phototoxic (foh-toh-TOK-sik) making the skin dangerously sensitive to sunlight

pollen (POL-uhn) tiny yellow grains that are part of a plant's process of reproduction

pollinate (POL-uh-nayt) to carry pollen from one flower to another, which fertilizes the second flower, allowing it to make seeds

resources (REE-sorss-iz) certain things living things need to survive, such as water or food

thatch (THACH) to cover a roof with straw, leaves, or another material

welts (WELTZ) raised red marks on the skin

Find Out More

Books

Lawler, Janet. *Scary Plants*. New York: Penguin Young Readers, 2017.

Miller, Connie Colwell. *The Deadliest Plants on Earth*. Mankato, MN: Capstone Press, 2010.

Thorogood, Chris. *Perfectly Peculiar Plants*. Lake Forest, CA: Words & Pictures, 2018.

Websites

The Alnwick Garden: The Poison Garden
   https://www.alnwickgarden.com/the-garden/poison-garden/

Chicago Botanic Garden: Peppers
   https://www.chicagobotanic.org/plantinfo/peppers_0

The Santa Barbara Botanic Garden: Invasive Plants
   https://www.sbbg.org/learn-discover/gardening-with-natives/invasive-plants

Index

About The Author

Joyce Markovics enjoys writing about and collecting unusual plants. One of her favorites is a burly South African clivia. It produces bright orange blooms in winter when many other plants are dormant.